MW01181745

JOURNEYS

JULIA WATERLOW

Thomson Learning • New York

Young Geographer

The Changing Earth
Food and Farming
Journeys
Natural Resources
Protecting the Planet
Settlements
The World's Population
The World's Weather

Front cover picture: Travelers with backpacks in Austria
Back cover picture: A man leading a camel in the desert in Tunisia
Frontispiece: A barge carrying cargo down the Rhure River

First Published in the
United States in 1993 by
Thomson Learning
115 Fifth Avenue
New York, NY 10003

First published in 1993 by
Wayland (Publishers) Ltd

Cataloging-in-Publication Data applied for

ISBN: 1-56847-051-7

Printed in Italy

Contents

All the words that are in **bold** appear in the glossary on page 30.

Introduction

The word journey comes from the French word *"jour,"* meaning day. Originally a journey was a day's work, or travel. Now it is used to describe any movement from one place to another.

Why do we make journeys? Are they necessary or do we just make them for pleasure? Think about the journeys you make. They will probably mostly be day-to-day journeys, like going to school or visiting friends. Occasionally you may have special outings or trips to visit places farther away.

The way we make journeys usually depends on where we live, how much time we have, and how far we want to go. Sometimes we go on foot, at other times by bus, train, or car. In some countries, people cannot afford to travel any way other than on foot or using animals. If transportation, such as a bus, truck, ship, or airplane, is available, it makes travel faster and easier. Transportation is especially helpful if we have to carry things with us or if we need to send goods to another place.

All over the world, people like these young Jamaicans use buses for everyday journeys.

Many years ago we did not have trains, cars, trucks, and airplanes. We have developed these efficient machines so that many people can travel quickly and take heavy loads with them.

However, so many people are now able to travel that roads and airways are becoming overcrowded and many journeys have actually become slower and more difficult to make.

Above *Even a simple vehicle makes carrying things easier. This Chinese man uses a tricycle to take his vegetables to market.*

Right *Traffic jams the crowded city of Tokyo in Japan. Above the cars a bullet train speeds across a bridge squeezed between buildings.*

Why we travel

Most of the trips we take are short distances, starting from home. These trips are regular, frequent, and usually do not take very long. The places people need to go to most often are usually nearby.

The main trip you probably take is to school. Perhaps you might also visit a local store on the way. After school you might go to join in sports or see your friends.

Sometimes you may go to the doctor or dentist, but these are usually local trips, unlikely to take a long time.

Many grown-ups also have to make short daily trips, usually to go to work or to go shopping. Some of them may have to travel farther to their workplace. When work is some distance from home, the people often have to use transportation such as

Every day young people all over the world have to make the trip to school. Often the distance is short, so they can walk.

Right Nowadays so many people commute into cities that big traffic jams result. This can mean that even short trips take a long time.

Below Underground or subway trains can move large numbers of people around quickly; but in some places they, too, become overcrowded.

cars and trains to **commute** into towns or big cities. Because so many people all move at the same time, the traffic becomes **congested** and the journey can take a long time, Finding a way of moving masses of people as quickly as possible has become one of the biggest transportation problems of our modern age.

Long-distance journeys, like those to the other side of the world, take only a few hours by plane.

Not all journeys are short, daily trips. Perhaps you can think of a time when you went on a long journey–perhaps on vacation to another country, or just for a day's **excursion** to another town. You may have traveled there by car, bus, or train. If you went abroad you may have traveled by airplane. Flying allows you to travel thousands of miles far more quickly than by other means of transportation.

Long journeys are not always just for pleasure. They are also made for work or business. A businessperson may have to fly to an important meeting in another country; a truck driver may have to carry goods across a **continent** to the sea; or a farmer may take pack animals through the mountains to a market far away. Others, like many of the workers in the oil-rich states around the Persian Gulf, have traveled

The Hussan Family

The Hussan family lives in a village in Egypt. There are three sons and two daughters in the family. Every day Mr. Hussan goes to work on his land a mile or so from home. He usually rides on his donkey, which he also uses to do heavy work like plowing the fields.

On most days Mrs. Hussan walks to the market to sell a few vegetables and to buy whatever food the family needs. The younger children also walk to school.

Their oldest son now lives about 60 miles away in Cairo, the capital of Egypt. He takes the bus to work everyday,

In Egypt, farmers ride their animals to go to and from the fields.

or if he is very late he goes by subway, which is quicker. Whenever there is a holiday, he goes home to his village by train. On New Year's, the whole family pays someone to take them in a van to visit their grandparents and cousins in a village not far away.

In remote areas where there are no roads, animals are taken to market on foot.

from distant countries to take up well-paid work for a few months or years before returning home.

Moving to a new home can sometimes mean a long journey perhaps to another part of the country, or sometimes abroad. People may move to get a new job or to go to a more attractive area to live. On **retirement**, older people often move to a smaller house or apartment, while some even go to another country if they think the weather and life-style are better.

Travelers

For most of us, a journey means going from home to another place. Some people, such as gypsies and **nomads**, live much of their lives traveling from place to place.

Gypsy travelers live in nearly every country of the world. They live in caravans, staying in one area for a few weeks–perhaps to get work at harvest time–and then move on. Nomads have homes, such as tents, that can be

transported fairly easily. Nomads often keep animals and move with them at different seasons to find better **pastures**.

Shepherds and cowherds drive their herds to find fresh mountain pastures in the spring and return to the lowlands at the end of summer. This seasonal migration is called transhumance. The Lapps of the Arctic, who traditionally herded

A nomad in Iran leads camels loaded with the family's possessions as they move to a new camp.

Shepherds like these in Morocco often move their flocks to new pastures at different seasons.

reindeer, were nomads who followed their animals when they migrated in search of food. But today, like many people who used to be nomadic, many Lapps lead a different, more settled life-style.

Some of the Bedouin–Arabs who live in the deserts of the Middle East and North Africa– still lead a nomadic life-style. Living in tents, they travel with a herd of camels, which they use to carry heavy loads. They survive by constantly moving around looking for grazing areas and water for their herds of camels, sheep, and goats. Other Bedouin travel by truck instead of camel and use trucks to carry all their animals and possessions.

A family group in Mongolia. The Mongols are herders. In summer they move their tents to fresh grazing lands.

Mongols

Many of the world's nomads, such as the herders of Mongolia, live in Central Asia. The Mongols inhabit an area where the land and climate make it difficult to grow any crops very successfully. However, there are grasslands and so they herd animals, usually sheep, cattle, goats, camels, or horses. By moving around, they can always find fresh grass for their animals. Most Mongol nomads move twice a year, from a summer pasture to a winter pasture.

Their homes are tents, called yurts, which can be taken down and carried easily. A wooden frame is covered with a thick layer of felt cloth. Inside they decorate their tents with rich, colorful rugs. The Mongols stay warm in the freezing winters by keeping a stove burning in the middle of the tent.

There are groups of people who make journeys so they can settle permanently in another area. They are called migrants. All through history, people have traveled enormous distances hoping that life in a different place will be better. For example, thousands of people have migrated to North America in the last hundred years, hoping for good opportunities to work.

Sometimes people are forced to make journeys. In the eighteenth and nineteenth centuries, millions of people from Africa were taken as slaves by Europeans to work in the Americas. In some countries today, people are forced to leave their homes and make journeys for different reasons. Perhaps they lack basic essentials like food and water. In the early 1980s, **drought** hit the African

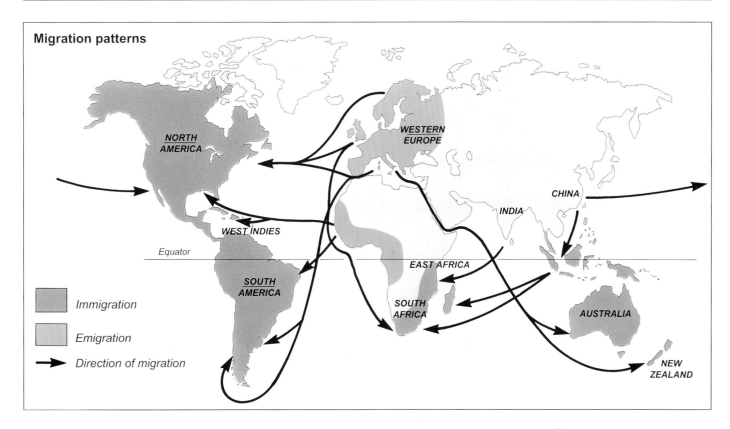

Migration patterns

NORTH AMERICA

WESTERN EUROPE

CHINA

INDIA

WEST INDIES

Equator

EAST AFRICA

SOUTH AMERICA

SOUTH AFRICA

AUSTRALIA

NEW ZEALAND

Immigration

Emigration

Direction of migration

A map showing where migration has occurred between 1850 and the early twentieth century.

countries of Sudan, Ethiopia, and Somalia. The people could no longer grow food, and, faced with starvation, they made long journeys in search of water and help.

Some of these journeys were made to escape the hunger and misery of **civil war**, which had a devastating effect on these areas. People who make journeys to escape natural and political troubles in the areas where they live are called refugees. Some return home later, but others stay away for good.

Many Vietnamese refugees have sailed to Hong Kong, hoping to escape troubles in their own country.

Making journeys

Think of all the different ways you or your friends could make the trip to school: on foot, by bicycle, by car, or perhaps by train or boat. There are many things that affect our choice of how to make a journey. The speed and cost of traveling may help people to choose. In developing countries, many people are too poor to buy their own cars, and there may not be a bus or train service, so they have to walk or go by bicycle.

For everyday trips, people take whatever form of transportation is nearest, quickest, and cheapest. It might not be worth going by car if there is only a short distance to travel, but it may be better than walking in bad weather. On a long journey it might be best to travel by train or a plane if it is important to arrive quickly. However, it is not usually possible to stop off on the way; and air and rail travel may not take you directly to the place you want to go.

Above *Across the huge distances and flat deserts of northwest China, trains provide an efficient way to carry people and goods.*

Left *In Tibet, many roads are tracks up steep mountainsides and it is possible to travel only by foot or by horse.*

Different kinds of transportation

Airplane
Fast (600 mph).
Expensive to build and run.
Can reach distant and remote places.

Helicopter
Takes off vertically.
Can hover.
Slower than airplane.

Animal
Can travel long distances.
Slow.

Double decker bus
Efficient.
Carries many people.
Arranged route.

Bicycle
Relatively slow.
No polluting fuel.

Subway
Quick across cities.
Often crowded.

Train
Fast (168 mph).
Requires efficient network.
Carries many people.

Sailboat
Used mostly for leisure.
Requires wind power.

Car
Convenient.
Polluting and expensive fuel.
Traffic jams.

Truck
Heavy loads carried directly.
Noisy.

Hovercraft, or
A.C.V. (Air Cushion Vehicle)
Fast (75 mph).
Restricted by weather.
Can go on water and land.

Cargo ships
Slower than by air.
Can carry heavy and bulky loads.
Need special terminals to unload.

Airship
Uses little fuel on long distances.
No need for runway.
Not very fast.

Both the local landscape and the weather have an affect on the type of transportation that people choose to use. In hilly areas, there are few railroads because trains cannot go up steep slopes. Areas of flat land are well suited to walking or cycling but usually only for short distances. In cold places where the land is covered by snow and ice, people may have to use sleds, skis, or **snowmobiles** to get around. In some parts of the world, near big rivers or their estuaries, boats are the only possible method of transportation, since roads too often become flooded.

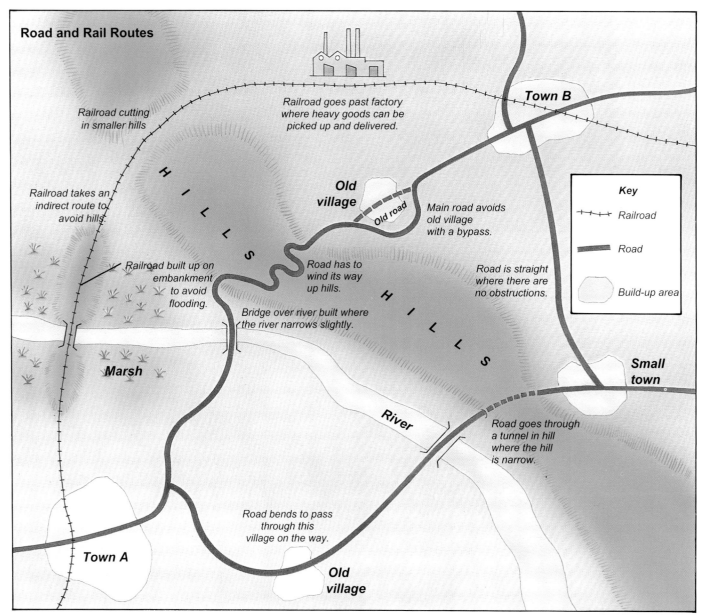

Road and Rail Routes

Railroad goes past factory where heavy goods can be picked up and delivered.

Town B

Railroad cutting in smaller hills

Old village

Old road

Main road avoids old village with a bypass.

Railroad takes an indirect route to avoid hills.

H I L L S

Key

＋┼┼＋ Railroad

Road

Build-up area

Railroad built up on embankment to avoid flooding.

Road has to wind its way up hills.

Road is straight where there are no obstructions.

H I L L S

Bridge over river built where the river narrows slightly.

Marsh

Small town

River

Road goes through a tunnel in hill where the hill is narrow.

Road bends to pass through this village on the way.

Town A

Old village

Right Lying at the mouth of a great river, Bangladesh frequently has floods, so boats become the easiest way to travel.

Left The type of country around us affects the way we are able to travel.

In Venice, gondolas ferry people along roadlike canals.

Venice

Venice is a city without roads or cars; it is built out on the sea on more than 100 islands. People travel by boat along canals, which twist and turn between the islands. The special boats in Venice are called **gondolas**. On the islands themselves there are narrow paved alleys where it is possible only to walk, not drive. Hundreds of bridges arch over the smaller canals.

Water transportation has always been the main means of traveling for Venetians. Hundreds of years ago, Venice became a great seafaring city, controlling trade in most of the eastern Mediterranean. Today, Venice makes most of its money from tourism. However, this may not be enough to save the city whose biggest problem is that it is slowly sinking into the sea.

Liquid cargoes such as oil are most easily and cheaply carried around the world in tankers.

Sometimes goods need to be carried on a journey. These goods are called **cargo**. Trains and ships are able to take large amounts of heavy and bulky goods much more cheaply than airplanes can. Oil, for example, is taken around the world in huge **supertankers**, and coal is transported across land by train. For less bulky goods, road transportation is often cheaper and quicker than rail because the goods can be delivered directly to the door. A wide variety of vehicles are

Huge trucks with several trailers carry goods on fast roads across long distances.

Freight Carriers

Heavy trucks are used as commercial vehicles to carry heavy loads long distances by road. Trucking is particularly common in the United States.

The vehicles are often articulated. This means that the power unit, or tractor, is separate from the trailer that carries the load. Trucks are usually powered by **diesel** engines with increased power from a turbocharger. Trucks may have as many as 20 gears forward and 6 gears to go backward. This allows the vehicle to cope with hills and to travel in all kinds of conditions. As the trucks are very heavy they need very powerful brakes.

Trucks may also have special machinery such as lifters, crushers, and hoists.

used, from light vans to heavy trucks. Some goods, such as flowers or special fruits, are flown by air because they would spoil on a long journey.

In many developing countries, animal transportation is still widely used to carry goods because it does not need expensive **fuel**.

Transportation

Way back in history, people walked wherever they wanted to go. Then animals were tamed, and people learned to ride on their backs. Goods were either loaded on or dragged along behind. The biggest change in land transportation came with the invention of the wheel. This led to the many forms of land transportation that have wheels.

For hundreds of years the invention of the wheel was enough to help people make the overland journeys they needed. Animals of all kinds pulled carts and wagons for goods, carriages for people, and chariots for war. Roads were built from one town to another, and inns and other stopping places sprang up along the main routes.

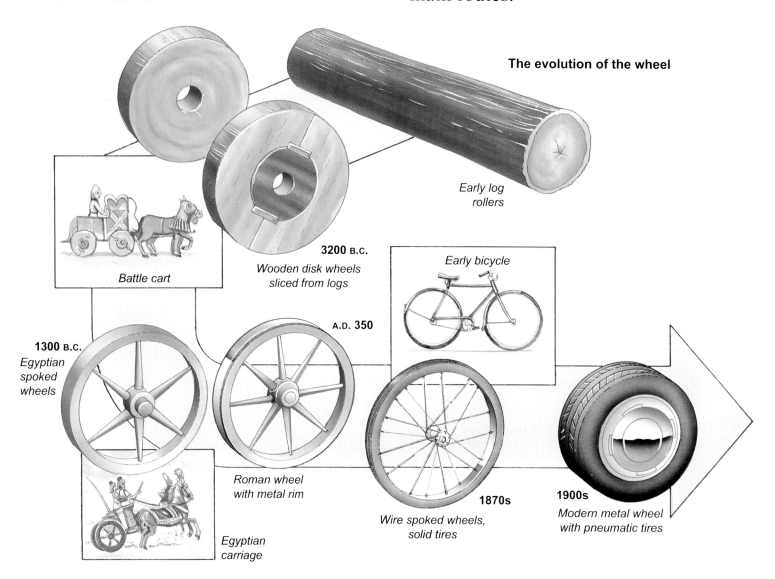

The evolution of the wheel

Early log rollers

Battle cart

3200 B.C.
Wooden disk wheels sliced from logs

Early bicycle

A.D. **350**

1300 B.C.
Egyptian spoked wheels

Roman wheel with metal rim

Egyptian carriage

1870s
Wire spoked wheels, solid tires

1900s
Modern metal wheel with pneumatic tires

Canals are artificial waterways built for carrying freight as well as leisure barges.

Water transportation was very important in opening up the world for trade, for exploration, and for conquering other lands. From simple paddled rafts, probably used for fishing or to cross rivers, ships powered by oars or by sail were developed, which could travel across seas. Special **docks** were built at ports to make loading and unloading goods easier. Inland, where there was enough water, canals were built to carry cargo from one place to another.

The Railroads

When George Stephenson completed the first public railroad in Britain in 1825, it was the beginning of a revolution in transportation. Although his steam train traveled at only 15 mph, large numbers of people could travel a relatively long distance comfortably and safely. Trains were also ideal for transporting heavy goods overland.

Railroad building started all over the world. A line was built across North America in 1869 opening up huge new areas of the continent. Britain built railroad **networks** in its colonies such as India, where they are still used today.

An early steam engine, built in 1813.

Even though steam trains could pull huge loads and the fastest set a speed record of over 124 mph, electric and diesel trains gradually took over because they were more efficient. Today the fastest trains are the TGV (*Train á Grande Vitesse*) in France and the bullet train in Japan. These **streamlined** electric trains both have to run on a specially built track because of their speed – the TGV regularly travels at 168 mph.

The TGV is the fastest train in the world, running between Paris and other big cities in France.

The Great Eastern *of 1857 was one of the early big seagoing steamships.*

The invention of the engine changed all this. The new railroad steam engines that were built could carry large numbers of people and goods and move them quickly from place to place. Steamships did not need to rely on wind and could make the big sea crossings more reliably than sailing ships. The invention of the internal combustion engine a century ago has now given people the freedom to travel wherever they want to quickly and comfortably by car. Finally, the development of airlines in the 1920s has now given people the ability to reach the other side of the world in hours.

Other types of transportation have also developed, and some are quite specialized. In the Arctic, boats called icebreakers are used to break channels in ice, and sleds are used to travel over the ice and snow. In crowded cities, underground train systems easily move huge numbers of people. To carry cargoes cheaply, container ships and huge trucks have been built. Hovercraft, or **ACV**s, are used to travel quickly over land and sea, and tanks are designed to grip difficult ground with their caterpillar tracks. Other forms of transportation have been specially developed for war, such as submarines and aircraft carriers.

On snow and ice, only special vehicles like this one, which has skis, can manage the difficult, slippery surfaces.

Because a helicopter can take off and land vertically, it does not need a runway.

The Helicopter

The helicopter is a nearly perfect flying machine. Although it is not as fast as some other flying craft, it is able to move in any direction and to hover in the air in difficult areas that other aircraft cannot reach.

Helicopters have a rotary blade that provides both the force to lift the machine and its flying propulsion. The helicopter can take off vertically, and by altering the amount of lift on the blades, the pilot can propel it an any direction. Sometimes there are twin rotors that turn in opposite directions.

Helicopters have many commercial and military uses and are particularly valuable for sea, ambulance, and mountain rescue work.

Journeys in the future

Over the last hundred years we have developed transportation to make our journeys faster, cheaper, and more comfortable. Now, because so many people are traveling, we have reached a point where our journeys, particularly by car, are actually getting slower. Think of the congestion in and around towns and cities all over the world. Traffic in New York City today sometimes averages the same speed as it did a hundred years ago!

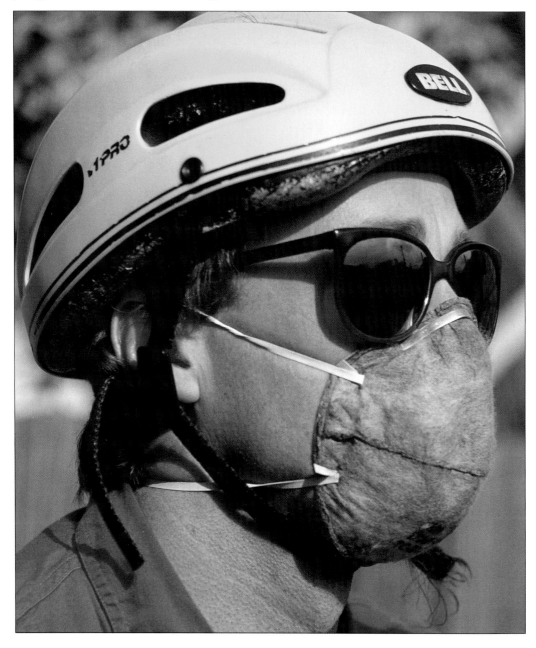

In many cities of the world car traffic is causing pollution; this cyclist wears a mask to avoid breathing in fumes on his journey.

More cars mean more and bigger roads. A huge area of land has been used to build this freeway interchange in Los Angeles.

The cost of road transportation actually is rising too because the fuels we use are becoming scarcer. There are also side effects. Gasoline has poisonous substances in it that **pollute** the air we breathe. New roads we build take up more and more land, often open countryside. As the roads become congested, there are more accidents.

Powerful magnets raise this maglev train off the track and propel it at high speed.

Some ways of dealing with the congestion are to extend our road network by building bypasses around towns, making one-way streets, and building overpasses. New roads are built, both with wider traffic lanes and with more lanes so that vehicles can move faster. What often happens, however, is that more people use the roads and the congestion is soon as bad as ever.

New **technology** can help by creating cars that use less fuel or cause less pollution. Technology is also changing other forms of transportation, such as trains. New maglev (magnetic levitation) trains which run just above a magnetic rail are being developed. There is little **friction** so they use less power than a normal train and are very quiet.

For longer distances, there are other ideas. Ships with computer-controlled sails as well as diesel engines have been developed, which saves on fuel. **Airships** are once again becoming more common. These helium-filled craft do not need a runway, use very little power taking off, and can travel a long way without refueling. In space, journeys to other planets and the stars may be made only if spaceships can be designed to run on nuclear fuel.

This tanker has sails as well as diesel engines; the sails can be used to save fuel.

New Technology in the Car

Car manufacturers are coming up with ideas for engines that use less fuel and produce less pollution. New designs for streamlined cars that are less resistant to air will also help to control the amount of fuel they use. Fuels themselves are being studied, and some of the harmful substances are beginning to be taken out of gasoline.

Other fuels, such as diesel, can be used to power our cars. Diesel engines last longer, and diesel is cheaper than gasoline. Several different types of electric cars have also been developed. They are much quieter than a normal car and do not pollute the air. Up to now they

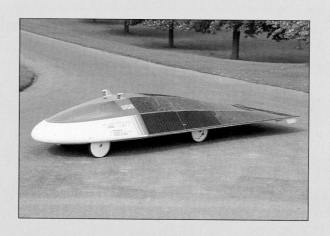

Solar cells collect energy from the sun to power the electric engine of this test car.

have not been successful because they cannot go very fast or very far – their big heavy batteries need recharging after a trip of less than 20 miles.

Technology, however, is unlikely to solve all the problems resulting from trying to move more and more people around. There may have to be controls restricting the use of cars. Already there are towns that ban cars completely from the city center. Making public transportation faster and more convenient would help to ease the traffic situation. To help solve the problem of pollution, many developed countries now limit the amount of lead in gasoline. It would also help to encourage people to use fuel-free transportation such as bicycles.

The modern bike is a very efficient way to travel. It needs no fuel other than leg power, and does not pollute the environment.

Glossary

ACV (air-cushion vehicle) A vehicle that rides over water or land on a cushion of air.

Airship A craft that is lighter than air, usually lifted by helium gas.

Cargo Goods to be carried.

Civil war A war between groups of people living in the same country.

Commute To travel regularly – usually between home and an office in town.

Congested Overcrowded as a result of too many vehicles or people packed together.

Continent A large land mass.

Diesel A type of heavy fuel oil.

Docks Places where ships can load and unload.

Drought A long period without rain.

Excursion A pleasure trip.

Friction The energy caused by rubbing one thing against another.

Fuel A material burned to provide power and energy.

Gondolas Long, narrow flat-bottomed boats propelled by a pole.

Maglev (short for magnetic levitation) A train that runs lifted off the rail. It uses the same forces that push magnets apart.

Migration The movement of people and animals from one place or region to another.

Network A pattern of roads or railroads that join each other.

Nomads People who have no settled home and move from place to place.

Pastures Land covered with grass that animals can eat.

Pollute To spoil or make dirty.

Retirement Giving up an active working life.

Snowmobile A motorized sled.

Streamlined Designed with smooth, flowing lines.

Supertankers Huge ships carrying liquid cargoes.

Books to read

Explorer, by Rupert Matthews. Eyewitness Books (New York: Alfred A. Knopf, 1991).

Rand McNally Classroom Atlas, rev. ed. (Chicago: Rand McNally, 1991).

Sailors: Ships and the Sea, by Richard Humble. Timelines (New York: Franklin Watts, 1992).

Transport: On Land, Road and Rail, by Eryl Davies. Timelines (New York: Franklin Watts, 1992).

Transportation, by Ian Graham. (New York: Hempstead Press, 1989).

Notes for activities

Think of somewhere you would like to go. Plan the route you would take to get there and think about how you would travel. Discuss with a friend why you are taking this route and the transportation you want to use. Alternatively describe a journey that you have already done and enjoyed.

Take two places near where you live or look on a map for two towns some distance away from each other. Look at the road that goes from one to the other. Draw a sketch map of the road and make notes as to why it takes the route it does. What physical features does it have to go over, under, or around?

Mark on a map where each person in your class lives. Ask each one how long it takes to get to school. With a line join together all those whose journey takes about the same time. Some people might live closer to school than you, but their journey may take the same time. Discuss why this is.

Imagine you want to send someone a letter. Write down each stage of the journey the letter will take and how it will be transported (by foot, bicycle, van, train, or plane.)

Find out all the different ways you could travel from the capital city in your own country to the capital of another. Make a list and look at the cost, the time, and how convenient each way is. Which have you chosen and why?

For one week, make a list of your friends' or family's journeys. Note why they are going, how they are traveling, and how long (in distance and time) it takes them. Afterward look and see if you can find a pattern of regular journeys.

Index

Picture acknowledgments

The publishers would like to thank the following for allowing their photographs to be reproduced in this book:
Cephas 7 bottom (Nigel Blythe), 25 (David Kirkman); Environmental Picture Library 26 (C.Martin);Mary
Evans 23; Eye Ubiquitous 4 (David Cumming), 14 both (Julia Waterlow), 19(Bennett Dean); the Hutchison
Library 13 bottom (René-Nicolas Giudicelli); Life File 10 (S.Kay), 22 bottom (Andrew Ward), Panos Pictures
6 (David Reed), 8 (Michael Harvey), 9 bottom (Jeremy Hartley),17 top (Trygve Blstad); Quadrant 28 (bottom);
Science Photo Library/Pacific Press 27 bottom; Tony Stone Worldwide *cover* (Ernst Hohne), *back cover* (Pete
Seaward), 5 bottom (Pete Seaward), 7 top (Ed Pritchard), 11 (Gerard Del Vecchio), 17 bottom, 24 bottom (P.
H. Cornut), 27 top, 29 (Gary Brettnacher); Wayland Picture Library 5 top (Richard Sharpley), 9 top, 21, 22
top; Zefa *frontispiece*, 12, 18, 28 top. Artwork is by Peter Bull.